GRUMPY CATS AND OTHER STUFF

A LITTLE STICKER BOOK

BY
CHARLOTTE FARMER

Skittledog

BEST
FRIENDS
MADE IN INDIA
DELUXE QUALITY
THE SUCCESSFUL STRIKE MATCHES

BEST MATCH

SAFETY MATCH
MADE IN JAPAN

SUPERIOR SAFETY MATCHES
MADE IN JAPAN

GOATHEAD
50¢
20's
DELUXE
BRILLIANT MATCHWORKS
WAX MATCHES

FANCY
WAX MATCHES

SAFETY
MATCHES
TRADE MARK
MADE IN JAPAN

ROYALDRAGON
575 SECOND AVENUE (NEAR 32ND ST.) N.Y.C.
AT UNIVERSITY CENTER

A MARINHA BRAZILIERA
PHOSPHOROS DE SEGURANÇA
FABRICADOS NA SUBCIA

THE TIGER
DAMP PROOF
MADE IN ITALY
SAFETY MATCHES

holiday
MOTEL
"Air Conditioned"

BEST SAFETY MATCH
日本製 MADE IN JAPAN

SUPERIOR SAFETY MATCHES
MAGIC MONKEY
MADE IN JAPAN

MADE IN JAPAN
BEST MATCH

SAFETY MATCHES
TRADE MARK
MADE IN JAPAN

SWAN MATCHES
MADE IN
SWEDEN

MADE IN JAPAN
LUCKYMATCH

S
GU

PIMENTON
ESPANA
MURCIA

Pimentón
PICANTE
SPANISH PAPRIKA
CABEZO DE TORRES

PIMENTÓN
LAS CARABELAS
HIJO de
JOSE Mª LOPEZ

PIMENTÓN
EL MONO
CARMEL FLORES

Gemaalde
WONDERPEPER

HUNGARIAN
PAPRIKA

PIMENTON
PURO
LOS DOS
CABALLOS
CABEZO DE TORRES

SZEGED PAPRIKA
RÓNA GYULA

PIMENTON
ESPINARDO
SPANISH PAPRIKA

PIMENTON EXTRA

PIMENTON
LA ARDILLA
MOLINA DE SEGURA

Pimentón
Garantizado
Puro
DiANA
Murcia España

Pimenton superior
picante
Espinado Murcia
Spain

PIMENT DOUX D'ESPAGNE
extra
Le Paradisier

PIMENTON
Pampera
Frutos del Pais
Spanish Paprika

PIMENTON
FELIXREVER
MURCIA ESPAÑA

PIMENT DOUX MOULU
"LE LION"
JOSEPH PUJANTE GOMARIZ
MURCIA ORAN ESPAÑA

GENUINE
IMPORTED
SAFE OWL
ROSE COLOR PAPRIKA
PACKED BY SAFE OWL PRODUCT, BROOKLY

CLASS C COMMON FIREWORKS
TIGER
BRAND
1½"
40s
SURE FIRE
FLASHLIGHT
CRACKERS
EXTRA LOUD
DO NOT HOLD IN HAND
CAUTION EXPLOSIVE
PLACE ON GROUND - LIGHT FUSE - GET AWAY

GROWLING
LION
1½ 20
THE
CRACKER
WITH A
BITE
BEST QUALITY
THUNDER FLASH CRACKERS
CAUTION: EXPLOSIVE
DO NOT HOLD IN HAND AFTER LIGHTING

DOUBLE HAPPY
"A SMALL CHAP
WITH A
LOUD VOICE"
7/8 x 1/6
40/80
DO NOT HOLD IN HAND
HIGHEST QUALITY
FANCY FLASHLIGHT CRACKERS
LIGHT FUSE - GET AWAY QUICKLY

CLASS C COMMON FIREWORKS
PANTHER
BRAND
WARRANTED HIGHEST QUALITY
FLASHLIGHT CRACKERS
CAUTION EXPLOSIVE
LAY ON GROUND - LIGHT FUSE - GET AWAY

PRESSED SUGAR
MODERN
AND
OLD FASHION
DANCING
Club
Flamingo

PIANO ENTERTAINMENT NIGHTLY
DELECTABLE DINING
THE NEW Plush Poodle
RESTAURANT and
COCKTAIL LOUNGE

Always A Friendly Welcome
TURF CLUB
CAFE & COCKTAIL LOUNGE

AUSTRALIA
Macropodidae
POSTAGE 8 1/2 D

বাংলাদেশ
SAVE THE TIGER
Panter tigris
৫০প 50P
BANGLADESH

中国邮政 CHINA
Ailuropoda melanoleuca
80分
GIANT PANDA

Guyana SOUTH AMERICA
POSTAGE & REVENUE

Postes
3
CENTIMES
CALEÇON ROUGE
REPUBLIQUE D'HAÏTI
Priotelus roseigaster

1ST
Kingfisher Alcedo atthis

MADAGASCAR
POSTES
PROTECTION DE LA FAUNE
12F
LEMUR CATTA MAKI

NIGERIA
Balearica pavonina
20k BLACK CROWNED CRANE

VIÊT-NAM
DÂN CHỦ CỘNG HOÀ
Tiger Shrike (Lanius tigrinus)
BUU CHÍNH
30 XU

St. LUCIA PARROT
St LUCIA

$1.50
SCARLET IBIS Eudocimus ruber
TRINIDAD & TOBAGO

AUSTRALIA
POSTAGE
GALAH
2 1/2 d.

COMMONWEALTH OF
DOMINICA
Sisserou Parrot
Amazona imperialis
60¢

EESTI POST
Canis lupus
Grey Wolf
1 MARK 1

Ursus arctos
2.00
SUOMI FINLAND

1 บาท
BAHT
POSTAGE
ประเทศไทย THAILAND

LION
Panthera leo
5/-
KENYA

Ciconia ciconia

CORREOS DEL PERU
ANDEAN
COCK OF THE ROCK

QATAR
10
RIYALS
Falco peregrinus
قطر

FELIS LYNX
Lynx lynx
POSTA ROMANA

REPUBLICA DE VENEZUELA
30c
VENEZUELAN TROUPIAL
Icterus icterus
Correo Aereo

PEOPLE'S DEMOCRATIC REPUBLIC OF YEMEN
50
FIL

Zimbawe 15c
SABLE ANTELOPE

HARBORSIDE
GRILL
2218 E CLIFF DRIVE
SANTA CRUZ

LE
PINGUIN
OPEN 7 DAYS A WEEK 5-10pm

LIGHTHOUSE
GRILL

BLACK CAT
LITTLE LUNCH

Top of the Ocean

La Fonda del Sol
West 50th St

THE ZEBRA
ROOM
AT THE Huntington HOTEL
GOOD FOOD AND COCKTAILS
SINCE 1974

MEET YOUR
FRIENDS
AT THE
BLUE BIRD
CAFE
PINE VALLEY, NY

Shore

39 Pier Fog Harbour
THE
OYSTER AND CHOPHOUSE

THE
POODLE DOG
1522 54th Ave E WA 98424
Family owned diner Since 1937

Le
Perroquet

HOTEL
Alameda
LA TAVERNA Cocktail Lounge

PureCane Sugars
A KIND FOR EVERY USE
Hotel
Raleigh

GASTHOF
Ambach

THE GALAXIE
MUSIC
DINING
DANCING
EXCELLENT
CUISINE

A
LOW NOISE

NR ON OFF
C-60

A

NR ON OFF

LOW NOISE

C-60

A

C90

100 50 0

Noise Reduction IN OUT

unbespielt unrecorded

A

C90

100 50 0

Noise Reduction IN OUT

unbespielt unrecorded

A

NR ON OFF

LOW NOISE

C=60

BACKHAND VOLLEY
A fine example of the backhand volley
· Move forward
· Don't let the ball drop
· Punch through the ball

FRED PERRY
WIMBLEDON WINNER 1934-6

LAWN TENNIS
FAMOUS FIGURES
Winner of 31 Grand Slam Tournament Titles
HELEN WILLS

"Jolly Well Played"

Short back swing
Stay down while hitting the shot
The only option when trapped by a ball at the feet

A difficult shot to control
Simply watch the ball all the time
BILL TILDEN

Short back swing
Stay down while hitting the shot
The only option when trapped by a ball at the feet

WHO'S WHO IN SPORT (1926)
"The Crocodile"
WORLD Nº 1 1926
RENE LACOSTE

ANYONE FOR TENNIS?

THE SERVE
The most important shot in the game
MISS PEGGY SAUNDERS

RETURN OF FAST SERVE
An unusual stroke requiring perfect timing
Sweep racket upward and slightly forwards
TENNIS MASTERSTROKES

PLATE 2

BIRDS OF THE WORLD

Turdus merula

Blackbird

PLATE 3

BIRDS OF THE WORLD

COMMON CANARY

Serinus canaria

PLATE 1

BIRDS OF THE WORLD

TANGARA CABANISI

Azure-rumped Tanager

PLATE 2

BIRDS OF EUROPE

Fringilla montifringilla

Brambling

BUNNY BLEND
MORNING CHEER
COFFEE
MAKES GOOD COFFEE EVERYTIME
NET WEIGHT ONE POUND

DELIGHTFULLY REFRESHING
ORANGE PEKOE
"SIMPLY SUPERIOR"
TEA
ONE QUARTER POUND NET WT.

ONE POUND NET WEIGHT
BREAKFAST
DELIGHT
STEEL
CUT
COFFEE
FOR A CUP BEYOND COMPARE

TIGER
THE FINEST TEA IN THE WORLD
EXTRA FANCY ASSAM
NET WEIGHT
½ LB
TEA

"SPEAKS FOR ITSELF"
PURE
BREAKFAST
COCOA

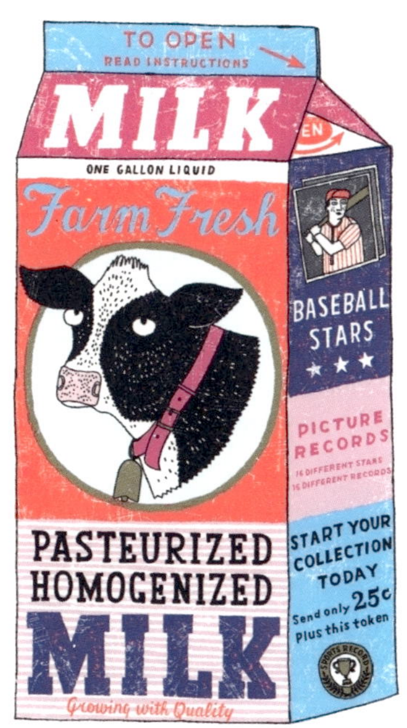
TO OPEN
READ INSTRUCTIONS
MILK
ONE GALLON LIQUID
Farm Fresh
PASTEURIZED
HOMOGENIZED
MILK
Growing with Quality
BASEBALL
STARS
PICTURE
RECORDS
16 DIFFERENT STARS
16 DIFFERENT RECORDS
START YOUR
COLLECTION
TODAY
Send only 25c
Plus this token
SPORTS RECORD

Big Cat
SUPER POWER
For
TRANSISTOR RADIO

EAGLE
9V
HEAVY DUTY
Guaranteed
BATTERY

Big Cat
Photo Flash
Battery
SUPER POWER
LEAK PROOF

SKY ROCKET
TIGER TORNADO
NEVER HOLD IN HAND

NO. 0925
GOLDEN
SUNRISE
EMITS SHOWERS OF SPARKS
LIGHT TOUCH PAPER · GET AWAY

KING
OF THE
SKY
FLIES AWAY · SHOOTS SPARKS AND HOWLING BALLS OF FIRE
EXTRALOUD

NIGHT OWL
SIZE 4
DRAGON CANDLE
EMITS SHOWERS OF SPARKS
DO NOT KEEP LOOSE FIREWORKS IN POCKET
CLIMBING PANDA
WARNING EXPLOSIVE
D.O.T
CLASS "C"
COMMON
FIREWORKS
HAPPY MOON
MUST NOT BE HELD
Whistling Fountain
WARNING: FLAMMABLE
SHOOTS SPARKS AND WHISTLES

FLYING CRANES
EMITS SHOWERS OF SPARKS AND WHISTLES

Midnight Panther
BRAND
THUNDER
ROCKET
DO NOT USE NEAR PEOPLE
WARNING - FLAMMABLE - LIGHT BLU

NO. 0623
J
OF
EXCITEMENT
MINE OF SERPENTS

LIGHT FUSE AND GET AWAY
GRIZZLY
GLITTERING FOUNTAIN
SHOOTS CRACKLING BALLS OF FIRE AND WHISTLES

ENSURE FIREWORK WILL NOT FALL OVER
EMITS SHOWERS OF SPARKS
TIGER TAILS
DO NOT HOLD IN HAND

First published in the United Kingdom in 2026
by Skittledog, an imprint of Thames & Hudson Ltd,
6–24 Britannia Street, London WC1X 9JD

Designer: Alison Guile
Production: Felicity Awdry

EU Authorized Representative: Interart S.A.R.L.
19 rue Charles Auray, 93500 Pantin, Paris, France
productsafety@thameshudson.co.uk
www.interart.fr

A CIP catalogue record for this book is available from the British Library

ISBN 978-1-83776-117-3
01

Printed and bound in China by Starlite